VEGAN BODY BUILDING DIET

Includes 50 Vegan Recipes that will help you build muscle and feel healthier

Mariana Correa

Certified Sports Nutritionist

Copyright Page

2015 Vegan Bodybuilding Diet

ISBN

Acknowledgement

To my family, thank you for your support and love throughout the years. Everything I have achieved has been thanks to you. I am forever grateful.

About the author

Mariana Correa is a certified sports nutritionist and former professional tennis player.
Mariana reached a career high of 26 in the world in juniors with wins over Anna Ivanovich (former #1 WTA in the world) and many other top 100 WTA players.

She competed successfully all over the world in over 26 countries and hundreds of cities including in London for Wimbledon, Paris for the French Open and in Australia for the world championships. She also represented Ecuador in Fed Cup, where the team reached the finals in their group.

During her career she was awarded the fair play award many times, proving to be not only an excellent player, but also a role model for other athletes.

Being an athlete herself she understands what it takes to be the best in what you love.

Mariana is a certified sports nutritionist with years of experience in proper nutrition and hydration for high performance athletes.

She combines her love and knowledge in sports and nutrition in this book to provide you with all the information you need to succeed.

Description

Vegan Bodybuilding Diet is the best book for anyone who is looking to build more muscle, train harder and feel healthier.

You will only achieve your goals if your body is healthy from the inside out. You will improve your performance through eating the right foods for you. This book includes a clear explanation of what you need to succeed and includes over 50 easy vegan recipes that will set you on the path of your best performance.

Your connection with food is the biggest influence for your long-term well-being. The first thing to consider when you would like to make a change in your life is your diet. A healthy nutrition is the foundation of your strength training program and athletic development.

The author Mariana Correa is a former professional athlete and certified sports nutritionist that competed successfully all over the world. She shares years of experience both as an athlete and a coach bringing a priceless perspective.

Enjoy this book with vegan desserts, vegan breakfasts, vegan dinners, vegan snacks, vegan lunches and more.

Table of Contents

Introduction

Achieve your Best Weight

"Most people have no idea how amazing their body is designed to perform" Mariana Correa

Most people believe being vegan means eating nothing but lettuce and tomatoes. At first they try eating only broccoli one day, then only carrots the next. By day three their goals and diet are out the door. With this book you will learn there is so much more to a vegan diet than carrots and broccoli.

There is such a great variety in a vegan diet and you don't need to be a professional chef to achieve your goals either. In our last chapter you will find 50 great recipes for weight trainers that are simple, affordable and easy to prepare.

Let's begin by understanding your body is perfection. Yes, no matter what you think it's perfect. Every single cell works together in synchronicity allowing you to be healthy and perform your everyday activities and training.

Do you have any idea of all the cells that are working together in order for you to read this book or something as simple as the process of breathing? Your body is incredible, but in order to stay in top shape it needs your help.

An active lifestyle combined with good nutrition is the best way to stay healthy.

Nutrition is eighty percent habit. You most likely have had the same nutritional habits for years and years. It will take time, discipline and constant support to change your habits and reach your potential.

In our current time sports are becoming even more demanding than ever. Athletes need to be stronger, fitter and faster. And a good training program by itself won't even get you midway to the body you need to be the best.

Yes, it's absolutely necessary to have a great training program and without it you won't accomplish much, but any champion can tell you that the single most important factor in creating the ultimate body is a proper nutrition plan.

There is only enough room at the top for the ones who really want it.

Nothing will ever come for free or granted. Do you love it enough to fight day in and out to reach your goals?

Yes! Wonderful, then let's get started.

Chapter 1

Vegan Enlightened

The first question that needs to be answered is what exactly it means to be on a vegan diet.

Vegans do not eat meat, fish or poultry. In addition to this, vegans do not use any animal products or by-products such as dairy products, leather, fur, silk, wool, cosmetics, eggs or anything derived from animal products. So in conclusion, unless it's plant derived, it's a no-go.

Why exactly do vegans adapt to these conditions? There are many reasons why vegans make this choice :

- The main aim why many chose veganism is due to moral reasons. By consuming animal products one is inevitably contributing to the demeaning conditions in which most animals spend their lives before being consumed.

- Another reason for veganism is health. Vegan diets are diverse, with richness in fresh, colorful and nutrient dense foods. Which promote overall better health as well as an enhanced performance for athletes.

- Others simply do not enjoy the taste of meat or animal products such as milk or eggs.

Whatever your reasons are this book will guide you in the right direction. People who make the switch from a normal diet to a vegan diet will see big changes right away. This will sound very appealing to those with health issues. For example if you have high blood pressure, this will decrease; if you're overweight you may shed those unwanted pounds quicker.

The best way to succeed in this diet is to understand that at the beginning this transition will not be easy. The road to a healthy lifestyle is paved with many temptations. It helps to have a support group, friends or family who will help you along the way.

Another key to success is to do your homework. Make sure you read the labels on the products you consume and use to make sure they are vegan.

Vegan History, How it all Began

The beginning of veganism has a foundation as early as the 1800s around the world. But officially in the U.S.A. the concept began as early as 1944 in North America, but it wasn't until 1949 when Leslie J Cross properly defined veganism. The concept began as a simple concept as "The principle of the emancipation of animals from exploitation by man."

Ultimately the definition of veganism was further illuminated by the American Vegan Society in 1979 as:

"A philosophy and way of living which seeks to exclude- as far as is possible and practicable- all forms of exploitation of, and cruelty to, animals for food, clothing or any other purpose; and by extension, promoted the development and use of animal-free alternatives for the benefit of humans, animals and the environment. In dietary terms it denotes the practice of dispensing with all products derived wholly or partly from animals."

Fast forwarding to this day and age this concept has remained true to vegans all around the world. There is a greater availability of vegan foods at supermarkets allowing for even more variety in the vegan diet.

In the following chapter we will discuss in depth what can be consumed in the vegan diet.

Chapter 2

Vegan Foods

"You don't have to be great to start, but you have to start to be great." Zig Ziglar

Most people have the misconception all they can eat is lettuce and tofu as a vegan, which comes as a surprise to me in this day and age with the wealth of information available.

The vegan diet consists of only plant-derived foods. This doesn't mean you'll be breaking the bank or eating fancier meals. The most inexpensive and nutritious vegan foods can be found all around you, from your backyard, the farmers market and your local supermarket. From fresh produce, grains, legumes, fruits, nuts and seeds to now available vegan cheeses, desserts, veggie burgers and much more.

A healthy and balanced vegan diet contains these food groups:

1. Grains
2. Vegetables

3. Fruits
4. Legumes, Seeds and Nuts

The amounts and combinations of each of these mentioned here will serve as a blueprint since each individual is unique the precise amounts for each will vary according to age, weight, health conditions, and nutrient and energy requirements.

1. Grains- these provide us with fiber, minerals, proteins, and antioxidants. Our goal is to consume mostly intact whole grains such as oats, brown rice, and millet. The amount of daily servings varies on your individual needs.

2. Vegetables- these are a huge part of the vegan diet. By consuming a wide variety of vegetables you can make sure your body will be receiving an assortment of necessary vitamins and minerals.

3. Fruits – these provide us with fiber, vitamins and a vast amount of antioxidants. Ideally we get a full

amount of vitamins from fresh fruits instead of fruit juices or frozen fruits.

4. Legumes, Seeds and Nuts – a vast amount of the daily required amount of protein will become available in this food group. This group includes legumes such as split peas, beans, lentils, and more. It also includes seeds such as sunflower seeds, pumpkin seeds, quinoa, and more.

In addition to this vegans can consume many foods that many others are familiar with. Such as hot dogs, burgers, ice cream, and cheese. These familiar foods have been adapted to a vegan diet by substituting animal products with alternatives such as a veggie burger, a coconut ice cream, a vegan hot dog and many more.
Vegans enjoy many of the same foods as other diets do, such as chips and salsa, pasta, and most breads are also vegan.

For many these changes can be tough at the beginning, but with simple substitutions you can easily switch to a vegan diet. Let's see some simple substitutions that can help you with this transition:

Cow's milk is probably one of the easiest to substitute with so many plant based alternatives now available in the supermarkets.

- Soy milk is extremely healthy and some brands will even fortify it with protein and vitamin D.

- Rice milk is made from the liquid of crushed rice with a light taste and contains similar amounts of calcium as cow's milk.

- Almond Milk this milk is ideal for desserts and baking, is high in healthy fats.

- Oat Milk contains a high amount of fiber and iron and is very easy to make. By simply leaving rolled oats soaking in water overnight, blend, strain and voila.

- Coconut Milk is low in calcium and in calories but still packs in protein, vitamins and minerals. Creamer texture allows for creamy sauces and desserts.

Cheese: Companies that make our milk alternatives also tend to make cheese and yogurt from these milks. You can find an interesting variety of cheeses for melting or ricotta or cottage cheese with these milks as well.
- Soy cheese is specially a great alternative as it melts and tastes just like cow's milk.

Eggs: There are many alternatives for eggs, depending on what kind of meal you're preparing, whether it's sweet or salty you have many options. Among these are:

- Apple sauce is a creative alternative, with only ¼ cup needed to replace one egg.

- Ground Flax seeds will provide you with a healthy amount of Omega-3 fats and fiber. I would recommend this option mostly with baked goods.

- Tofu provides a nutritious amount of protein in similar amounts as an egg would. Tofu is a great alternative for heavy egg recipes such as scrambled eggs, quiche and omelets.

Meat: Letting go of animal meats has never been easier. Companies are making so many products such as veggie meatballs, veggie bacon, veggie sausages, soy chicken patties and many more. If you would still like to use substitutes for your favorite recipes here are some alternatives:

- Tofu: with ½ cup of tofu packing a whopping 10 grams of protein this is a great meat alternative. Feel free to mix in some ground flax seeds to add some texture, since tofu's texture tends to be light and fluffy.

- Garbanzo beans contain as much as 12 grams of protein in a cup. They can easily be cooked, mashed and shaped into your favorite meals.

- Ground walnuts or almonds are perfect for when you need to add texture to any recipe, allowing for a more chewy and crunchy feel in every bite.

Honey: Some vegans that aren't very strict with their diet and will consume honey, but in this case I am offering you a wonderful vegan alternative as is:

- Agave syrup: This plant based syrup is sweeter than honey so a little goes a long way. It's a fantastic option for smoothies, tea, desserts and more.

- Maple syrup is lower in calories than honey. Ideally you will purchase a less processed maple syrup to enjoy its full flavor. Maple syrup is full of zinc, iron, and many other minerals.

Chocolate: If you've got a sweet tooth as I do, there is no way you could ever give up chocolate. Luckily you don't have to. There are many non-dairy vegan chocolates, powders, and even chocolate bars.

Ice Cream: With all the milk alternatives available, you can easily find or even make ice cream with a nut base, rice base, coconut base and more. You can even opt for a fruit sorbet sweetened with agave. Even the kids will love it!

Try it

Yes, you could just give up now and say there's no way you can do this. But if you're looking for a healthier body and lifestyle then at least try it.

Before you go on to say how hard this is going to be for you, think about all the benefits that will come from it. Nothing but good things will come from this change in your life.

Start small begin by minimizing grains, sugar and processed foods gradually and see how your body feels.

When I began I thought of how much I loved eating croissants, and cheese sandwiches, but began slowly pulling away from these foods. Pretty soon I noticed that I was no longer missing these foods and even noticed they did not sit well with me, I felt bloated and fatigued after eating them

Begin with 30 days of complete discipline. After 30 days your body will begin to adjust from fueling itself on carbs and sugar to using your stored fat for energy.

The closer you shift your diet to vegan principles, the quicker you will begin to see and feel the results. Let's get started!

Chapter 3

Feed your body only the Best

"Because we are what we eat we can literally transform our bodies and minds by choosing an inspiring diet." M. Adams

Could eating a right meal make a difference in your performance? Of course!

Feeding your body properly is crucial to performing at a top level. Your body runs on whatever you feed it. Your meals are your fuel. If you want your body to perform at its full potential, you must keep it perfectly fine tuned.

When feeding yourself it's important to educate yourself about the meals you are eating, and how will these benefit your body. Ideally you would like to have a healthy, well rounded and complete diet. Remember these healthy habits you are instilling will carry on throughout your life. Later on you will be very proud of what you have accomplished.

Take a top athlete for example, do you think they indulge in chips and junk foods and perform better. They understand these foods will actually decrease their performance level so they avoid these foods, perhaps in a special occasion they will consume them, but they certainly do not consume junk foods as a habit.

Let's take Novak Djokovic for example a famous tennis player and currently #1 in the world. Several years ago he was a great tennis player, but faced several issues that wouldn't allow him to perform his best tennis. When playing long matches, he would often feel fatigued, sluggish, cramp up and on occasion throw up. He soon realized his issues were nutrition related.

He changed his diet completely and after only a couple of months he was in the best shape of his life and winning grand slams.

"My life changed because I had begun to eat the right foods for my body, and in the way that my body demanded… it changed my life really in a positive way and affected positively my career and my overall feeling on and off the court." Novak Djokovic.

His dedication was so clear that even after winning the Australian Open a major grand slam he craved chocolate after his win and after not eating a chocolate for 18 months he ate only one square and left the rest.

This kind of dedication is not easy to accomplish, but if you truly dream of your body and mind reaching its full potential you must sacrifice your cravings and usual habits.

- It's about making the right choices. The nutritional choices you make every day affect your health and performance. The better educated you are, the better choices you can make.

- It's about balance. You need to make time and space in your life for things that make you happier, healthier and more productive.

- It's about a healthier lifestyle. To get make the most of your body start with small steps, a steady and balanced approve on being healthy you can live with every day or at least most days. Hey, nobody is perfect.

Start today for a better tomorrow

How many times have you told yourself, "I will start eating healthier and training harder." And of course you mean well and you have every intention of following through with it, but you get derailed, one thing after another and you fall right back into your unhealthy habits.

Food has many meanings to us. For some it's a stress reducer, after a long day of work they're thinking of going home relaxing and comforting in a pint of ice cream. For others food is a way of celebrating special events or getting together with those we care about.

Make sure there are always healthy choices available to you so you can still enjoy yourself. Your true focus is in the day to day nutrition, the little things do add up and make a big difference.

Being on a diet doesn't necessarily mean you need to starve yourself, quite contrary it's all about eating, but eating all the right foods.

Good Calorie vs. Bad Calorie

So often we hear people mention calories in their food, what do they mean? A calorie is a unit of measurement of energy. Calories are Energy that fuel our bodies just like gasoline would fuel our cars. Without enough calories our heart would not beat, our brain would not function and our body could not survive.

When a certain food or beverage contains 100 calories it describes how much energy your body could get from eating or drinking it.

Not all calories are good calories. We will call the bad calories empty calories. The reason why we will call them empty is because they provide the calories, but offer no nutrients or nourishment for the body.

For example a banana is 100 calories, not only does it provide the calories but it also provides nutrients such as potassium, iron, Vitamin B6, phosphorus and more.

On the other hand we have a 100 calorie pack of chips, which is full of saturated fat, sodium, preservatives and offers no nutrients in exchange for its calories.

Although the 100 calories seem harmless as little calories equal to little weight gain and good health, it's safe to say that the amount of nutrients you consume are more important than a calorie amount.

Can we really compare 500 calories of spinach and vegetables with 500 calories in a soda with a burger? The nutrients provided in the spinach and vegetables will provide numerous benefits in your body and mind, while the empty calories will simply make you feel full temporarily.

Meanwhile the nutrients in the whole foods will signal your brain that you are full, the empty calories will have you soon after reaching out for more food.

RMR

On average an adult requires at least 1000 to 1500 calories to have enough energy to function. The energy would be first distributed to fuel essential organs such as the heat, brain and lungs. The minimum required number of calories is called the resting metabolic rate (RMR). And this number is unique for everyone as it depends on age, sex, weight and muscle mass.

We all have a RMR or Rest Metabolic Rate this would be the amount of calories or energy your body requires during the resting stage. This allows the body to fulfill the basic requirements the body needs to function properly. Calories are required to complete the essential body functions such as respiration, digestion, or heartbeat. Approximately 50 to 75% of an individual's daily energy requirements are credited towards the resting metabolic rate. Athletes tend to have a higher RMR because more calories are required to maintain lean body mass. To calculate the exact RMR you would need your exact height, age, weight and gender.

It's also very important to take into account the amount of hours the athlete is training.

The more hours of training, the more calories would need to be consumed.

It is a balance of nutrients that keeps athletes healthy and able to train hard for each session. Keep your future champion body healthy by choosing a variety of foods and keeping your plate colorful.

We mentioned above the more lean muscle the more calories need to be consumed calories due to faster metabolism. But we must provide our body with healthy calories, not empty calories. In the following chapter we'll go over what healthy options you should be choosing.

Chapter 4

Healthy Eating

"You are what you eat- so don't be easy, fast cheap or fake." M. Allen

Think you will go far in any sport by just doing the training and ignoring what you eat? Think again!

The proper nutrition is the foundation of health and performance, and in order to achieve your full athletic potential you must tune up your diet. What you ingest will greatly affect how you look, feel and perform, yet most athletes make their nutrition secondary in their training. Your nutrition affects you in every way possible, from your skin, your thoughts, your strength and speed.

Food quality

Before we begin to focus on portions and calories let's focus on the quality of your food. I want you to think about the last time you went to the supermarket, what aisles did you visit, what did you place in your cart?

I will let you in a secret, the next time you go to the supermarket focus ninety percent of your shopping on the perimeter of the grocery store. Only venture down the aisles for a few select foods like nuts, olives or canned tuna. If you realize the healthy foods are perishable therefore they are in the perimeters of the store. Unlike the aisles which are full of processed foods with ingredients you have no idea what they are and most of time can't even pronounce.

Healthy foods are perishable. They are organic plants and foods our bodies were built to consume. If a sugary cereal has a shelf life of several years, how good can eating that be for your body? It clearly has no organic material left, or it has been coated with enough chemicals to delay the decay. We now begin to wonder what effects those chemicals have on your body and mind. Many will say there is no evidence to sustain they do no harm, yet we know they do no good either.

Organic and Natural

Organic food has become a popular term lately. Years ago organic food was available only in health stores or in farmers markets, nowadays it has become widely available in many grocery markets.

What does organic mean? The term refers to the manner in which agricultural products are grown and processed.

In the beginning of farming all foods were organic. It was as simple as placing the seed in the ground and harvesting when ready. They were all grown free of pesticides and chemical fertilizers. Foods were minimally processed, unrefined and whole.

Today with the population growing, farming has taken a turn and tried to supply more and more with the help of pesticides and chemicals. This has made our foods not only deficient in nutrients, but also full of chemicals and toxins making it difficult for us to be healthy and well balanced.

In order to qualify as organic crops and livestock must be:

Organic crops must be grown in safe soil, have no modification or be genetically modified, and must remain separate from conventional food. Farmers are not allowed to use synthetic pesticides and petroleum or sewage based fertilizers.

Benefits of Eating Organic Food

- More nutrients. Several studies have shown that organically grown foods contain more nutrients than non-organic grown foods because the soil is sustained and nourished with healthy practices. The nitrogen that is found in composted soil is slowly released this way plants can grow at a normal rate, with their nutrients in balance.

- Better Taste. Many foods are now being modified to enhance their colors and achieve a more consistent shape. In return, the taste is not taken into account. Organic foods might not always be prettiest or shiniest, but they sure are the tastiest.

- Pesticide and chemical free. Research from the past few years demonstrate the negative effects of these toxins in our body such as cancer, asthma, brain function and more.

- Promote the local economy. Organic foods are quite often grown locally, visit your local market, you will probably get a better price and a fresher product.

- Organic Farming is better for the environment. These farms are sustainable, reduce pollution, conserve water and use less energy.

Cost vs. Health

This kind of grocery shopping will most likely be more expensive than you're used to. Fresh organic food costs more because it's real food. It will spoil quickly unlike processed foods which can be stored in boxes for months and still be edible somehow.

If you find buying fresh and organic to be too expensive for you can also opt for frozen meats, fruits and vegetables as an option.

Every year the EWG Environmental Working Group releases a list of 12 foods that you should always whenever available buy organic. It has been estimated individuals can decrease their exposure by 80% if they change to organic when purchasing those foods. The group analyzes which foods contain the highest pesticide residue and call those 12 the dirty dozen. Each year some foods change, but over the past couple of years these are the foods that have been on the dirty dozen consistently.

1. Strawberries
2. Grapes
3. Celery
4. Peaches
5. Spinach
6. Potatoes
7. Cherries
8. Lettuce
9. Cucumbers
10. Blueberries
11. Sweet bell Peppers
12. Nectarines

You must decide for yourself if eating this way is worth the cost. Personally I try to make cuts in other areas of my budget, but I find my health more important than anything else. Of course the bag of Cheetos is cheap and easy, but I am not willing to eat that when I have better options available.

Many of these changes might seem extreme from your current way of life. But if you want to improve your health and performance these changes are necessary.

You can choose to eat cheap and fast now and pay for it later or spend a little more on healthier food now but enjoy a better life on the long term.

Chapter 5

Macronutrients

"Anyone can work out for an hour, but to control what goes on your plate for 23 hours... now that's hard work." Anonymous

Nutrition is the most important characteristic in order to achieve your goals. Consider your body a fine-tuned Lamborghini and your muscles the engine. If you don't supply your engine with the correct fuel during a competition you won't perform half as well as your fine-tuned body could.

Even in your day to day life your body requires the correct kind of nutrition. If you know you're overweight by 10 pounds and think it's not that much try strapping on a 10 pound vest and see how well you perform with it on. Yes, those extra pounds will definitely hinder your performance.

Nutrition is different for each individual, and as such this is an overview of recommendations designed to help you as you plan your nutritional requirements for competing, training or for day to day meals.

Protein

Protein is a very important component in an athlete's diet, after all your muscles are made of protein. Protein is essential is promoting fast muscle recovery after workouts and to ensure your muscles adapt fully in response to your training, in order words, you start toning that body.

They are often called the building blocks of the body. Protein consists of a combination of structures called amino acids that combine in several ways to help create muscles, bone, tendons, skin, hair, and other tissues. Athletes need protein to assist in repairing and rebuilding muscle that was broken down during exercise. It also helps to optimize carbohydrate storage in the form of glycogen.

There are many doubts in this area, many believe that eating more protein will make you gain weight. When you train your muscles need to be replenished which is why they need protein to rebuild and restructure.

Athletes require more protein than individuals who don't train. If a sedentary person were to consume the same amount of protein an athlete consumes, then surely all the unused protein would turn into fat and weight gain would occur.

As long as you're training the protein you consume will repair your muscles and help you stay toned and healthy.

Research has proven that the timing of protein intake plays an important role. Eating high quality protein within two hours after exercising enhances muscle healing and development.
The length and intensity of the exercise is also very important when it comes to protein requirements. Power training needs a higher level of protein intake than endurance training does because power is focusing more on building muscle.

General Requirements
Research has proved the adequate intake of protein for improved athletic performance as 0.6 to 0.9 grams of protein per pound of body weight or 1.4 to 2 grams per kilogram. For example a 160 pound athlete requires 102 to 146 grams of protein per day.

As we mentioned above the intensity and purpose of training also make a difference in daily protein intake. We will review three possibilities below, endurance training, strength training and training to reduce fat.

- Endurance Training

According to the intensity of the training we could estimate that when training at a light to moderate regimen you would need 0.5 to 0.8 grams of protein per pound of body weight. When training in a high intensity regimen 0.7 to 0.9 grams per pound of body weight are recommended.

- Strength Training

It's recommended that when you are focusing on strength training in an intense regimen to consume 0.6 to 0.9 grams of protein per pound of body weight or 1.5 to 2.0 grams per kilogram of body weight. This amount is ideal to optimize muscle mass, strength and physical performance.

- Reduce Body Fat

When you are focused on reducing body fat but maintain your lean muscle mass the recommended protein intakes can be as high as 1.0 to 1.5 grams of protein per pound of body weight. These numbers can increase even more if you are restricting your calorie intake. Your goal at this time would be to maintain your lean muscles while burning off fat.

Where to find protein

Some examples of foods that contain protein are soy, legumes, lentil, beans, nuts and several vegetables such as avocado, cauliflower, asparagus, broccoli and artichoke.

My top recommendation for protein sources for athletes are:

Almonds

Protein is also found in plant foods such as nuts. It does not offer as much protein as animal foods, but when it comes to plant foods almonds are an excellent choice. Two ounces of dry roasted and salted almonds contains twelve grams of protein. Almonds also provide vitamin E, Fiber and much more.

Soy

Most likely the best plant source of protein. It can be found in many different ways such as tofu, edamame, soy milk, soy burgers, and soy protein based powdered drink mixes.

Protein Powder Hemp, Chia and Pea Blend

The closest there is to a perfect protein source. Commonly found in a variety of powdered drink mixes, nutrition bars, and more. Many studies have found that intakes of protein powder accelerate post-training recovery and enhance muscle performance.

Lentils

They are and easy and tasty way to consume a high dose of protein. With only ½ cup you will add 9 grams of protein and almost 15 grams of fiber to your meal.

Quinoa

There are incredibly versatile in many recipes and pack 8 grams of protein per cup. It also contains nine essential amino acids our bodies need for repair and growth.

Chia Seeds

With an impressive 5 grams of protein in 2 tablespoons, this little seeds pack quite a punch. They're easy to sprinkle on smoothies, salads and desserts.

Carbohydrates

They are the most important source of energy for athletes. No matter what sport you play, carbs provide the energy that fuels muscle contractions. Once carbs are consumed, they breakdown into smaller sugars that get absorbed and used as energy. A steady supply of carbohydrate intake prevents protein from being used as energy. The body stores carbohydrates as glycogen in the muscles and liver, but its holding capacity is limited. When the fuel needs of an athlete are not met with the stored carbohydrate the consequences include fatigue, reduced ability to train hard, impaired thoughts, and a decrease in immune system function.

For these reasons, athletes should plan their carbohydrate intake around key training sessions and their day to day requirements with carbohydrates as an exercise fuel.

Your carbohydrate requirements depend on the fuel needed in your training and competition program. The exact amount is dependent on the frequency, duration and intensity of the activity. Since your activities will change every day your carbohydrate intake should fluctuate to reflect this. On days with high activity carbohydrate intake should be increased to match the increase in activity. This increase will allow your body to maximize your activity and promote recovery between sessions.

On the other hand on low or no training days carbohydrate intake should be decreased to reflect the decrease in activity. A smart way to regulate carbohydrate intake from day to day is to schedule foods that are carbohydrate rich at meals or snacks around important activity sessions. As the intensity of the sessions increase you should increase your carbohydrate intake before, during or after exercising. This not only helps to have the proper amount of carbohydrates, but also it improves the timing so it's best suited to fuel the session.

The following numbers are a good standard to go by:

Light Training: Low intensity. 3-5 grams per kilogram of body weight.

Moderate Training: Average activity for approximately 1 hour. 5-7 grams per kilogram of body weight.

Intense Training. High intensity activity for 1-3 hours per day. 6-10 grams per kilogram of body weight.

Extreme training. Very high intensity activity for more than 4 hours per day. 8-12 grams per kilogram of body weight.

Simple and Complex Carbohydrates

Carbohydrates are both simple and complex.

Simple carbohydrates have a smaller structure with only 1 or 2 sugar molecules. Some simple carbohydrates include sucrose, sugar found in candy, soda, juice. They are the fastest source of energy, as they are quickly digested, but only last for a short period of time. They tend to have little or no vitamins and minerals.

Complex carbohydrates are made of many sugar molecules looped together like a necklace. They are commonly rich in fiber, and health promoting. Complex carbohydrates are usually found in whole plant foods and, hence, are also often full of vitamins and minerals. Examples would be cassava, yam, white potato, green vegetables, peas, sweet potatoes, pumpkin and other vegetables.

My top 5 recommendation for carbohydrate sources for athletes are:

Sweet Potatoes

One of my favorite carbohydrates since it provides so many nutrients in each bite. They are very high in antioxidants and potassium which helps sooth sore muscles. One cup equals 27 grams of carbs.

Berries

You name it, strawberries, blueberries, blackberries, and other berries are among the most nutritious sources of carbohydrates. They are not the most concentrated source of carbohydrates with only 12grams in one cup but they are extremely rich in vitamins, minerals and phytonutrients.

Bananas

The most common snack for athletes is easy to digest and loaded with fast acting carbohydrates. Bananas are a great pre or post exercise snack with 31 grams of carbohydrates.

Chestnuts

They are a great snack that provides quite a bit of fiber, vitamin C and folic acid. Chestnuts can be served roasted, in soups, stuffing and many more ways. Compared to other nuts chestnuts provide less than one gram of fat per ounce.

Oranges

They are an excellent option instead of bananas. One orange alone contains all the daily vitamin C requirements. Opt for the fruit instead of the juice so you can enjoy the benefits of the fiber as well.

Healthy Fats

Contrary to popular belief eating fat does not make you fat. It's the kind of fat you choose to eat that can make you fat.

Fat is one of the 3 macronutrients together with protein and carbohydrates that supply calories to the body. Fat provides 9 calories per gram which is more than twice the number offered by protein or carbohydrates.

Fat is actually one of the critical nutrients for optimal health and is essential for the proper functioning on the body. Fats provide essential fatty acids not made by the body and must be attained from food.

Omega-3 and Omega-6 fatty acids are required for normal growth and development and for the standard functioning of the brain and nervous system. Fat is the main storage source for the body's extra calories. It fills the fat cells that help insulate the body and it is also an important energy source. Fat is a fuel source for low-level to modest exercise such as walking or jogging, and is very important for extended endurance trials that are at lower intensities. After the body has used up all the calories from the carbohydrates consumed which normally occurs in the first 20-30 minutes of exercise it begins to rely on the calories from fat.

While fat is easily deposited in the body and is calorie-dense, it also takes longer to breakdown and digest. It can take up to 6 hours to be converted into a usable form of energy. This would clearly identify fat unsuitable as a pre- exercise snack and is why we choose carbohydrates to fuel our activities.

When consuming, choose "good fats" such as polyunsaturated and monounsaturated fats which are found in nuts, seeds, canola and olive oils, flax seeds and avocados.

Do not eat foods with "bad fats" such as potato chips, ice cream or any solid fat. They contain trans fats and saturated fats. Too much of these have been linked to health problems such as obesity, high cholesterol, heart disease and poor athletic performance.

Fats should represent no more than 25% to 30% of your total calorie intake. High-fat foods must be avoided as they can cause uneasiness if eaten too close to the start of physical activity. No consumption of trans fats and saturated fats. Emphasize healthy fats that are found in avocados, canola oil, soy, and nuts.

My top recommendations for fat sources for athletes are:

Flaxseed oil

We often cook with oils, and use oil in our salads and day to day meals, why not use oil that includes many of the same benefits as fish oil including a high level of Omega 3s. It's important to note that consuming flaxseeds alone we will not intake the same amount of omega 3s, flaxseeds must be ground up to release its fat content.

Avocados

Avocados are high in fat, but most of the fat in an avocado is in fact monounsaturated which is the heart-healthy kind that helps lower bad cholesterol. They make an excellent substitution for butter or cream cheese when needed.

Nuts

Walnuts, almonds, sunflower seeds, pistachios and pumpkin seeds are all very special nuts. They contain nutrients such as selenium, lutein, and are very high in vitamin E. Many of them are high in Omega 3 or Omega 6, they provide a good amount of fiber and are great for on the go snacks.

Chapter 6

Micronutrients

"You are given the opportunity to nourish your body with every bite and sip you take." M. Correa

Vitamins are vital elements that must be consumed because the body does not produce them by itself. They are essential to maintain healthy and balanced body functions.

Fruits and vegetables contain vitamins, minerals and antioxidants that are essential to maintaining a healthy and balanced diet. Examples are: Oranges, a great source for vitamin c, bananas for potassium, and carrots for beta carotene.

Two important minerals to consider in athletes are Calcium and Iron. Calcium helps build stronger bones, which decreases the chance of them breaking under stress or heavy activity. You can find calcium in many dairy products, such as milk, yogurt, and cheese. Also include dark, green leafy vegetables and calcium-fortified products, like orange juice as good sources of calcium.

Now we'll go into several important vitamins and minerals and better understand how they help us and where we can find them.

Vitamin A

Well known for proper vision development, it also has many other benefits. It maintains red and white blood cell production and activity. Promotes a healthy immune system, and keep skin healthy.

An optimal daily intake for a male would be 900 micrograms and for a female would be 700 micrograms.

Good sources of Vitamin A are squash, sweet potato, carrots, kale, apricot, peaches, cantaloupe, papaya, and mango.

In order to reach your optimal daily intake these foods contain a good amount of Vitamin A. It's important to remember that many vegetables loose many vitamins and nutrients when cooked.

Kale ½ cup = 443 mcg

Carrots ½ cup = 538 mcg

Cantaloupe ½ melon = 467 mcg

Spinach ½ cup = 573 mcg

Sweet Potato ½ cup = 961 mcg

Vitamin C

Vitamin C is essential for the biosynthesis of collagen. Collagen is the main protein used as connective tissue in the body. Collagen is especially important for healthy joints, ligaments, and bones. Other benefits of vitamin C include a boost in the immune system, supports in wound healing and improves brain function.

An optimal daily intake for a male or female would be 45 to 75 micrograms.

Good sources of Vitamin C are citrus fruits, leafy greens, peppers, and cauliflower.

In order to reach your optimal daily these foods contain a good amount of Vitamin C.

Red pepper raw ½ cup = 95 mcg

Orange juice ¾ cup = 93 mcg

Broccoli cooked ½ cup = 51 mcg

Kiwi fruit = 64 mcg

Strawberries ½ cup = 49 mcg

Vitamin D

Vitamin D is vital for proper calcium metabolism. Bone density is linked directly to this vitamin, as well as a good nervous system function and immunity.

This vitamin is a special one, it allows your body to manufacture Vitamin D when you get sunlight on your skin. No need to bask in the sunlight, no more than few minutes a day are required.

Vitamin D is not easily found in food in nature, which is why many products are now fortified with this Vitamin such as soy milk and orange juice.

An optimal daily intake for a male or female would be 15 mcg.

Vitamin E

Vitamin E is also called the excellent vitamin. It pertains to a family of eight antioxidants and as such protects our bodies from damage. Constantly battling free radicals protects essential lipids and maintains the balance of cell membranes. Naturally an anti-inflammatory, it aids in muscle wellness.

An optimal daily intake for a male or female would be15 micrograms.

Good sources of Vitamin E are nuts, seeds, avocado, wheat grains, and oils.

In order to reach your optimal daily these foods contain a good amount of Vitamin E.

Wheat germ oil 1 tablespoon = 20 mcg

Sunflower seeds 1 ounce = 7.4 mcg

Peanut butter 2 tablespoons = 2.9 mcg

Almonds roasted 1 ounce = 6.8 mcg

Vitamin K

The K in vitamin K is from German origin for "Koagulation" which means coagulation in German. This vitamin is essential for coagulation in our bodies. Deficiencies are visible with easy bruising, nosebleeds, and heavy menstrual periods.

An optimal daily intake for a male would be 80 mcg or female would be 65 micrograms.

Vitamin K is readily available in many foods we eat day to day, but is especially concentrated in leafy greens.

Kale ½ cup = 531 mcg

Spinach ½ cup = 444 mcg

Broccoli 1 cup = 220 mcg

Swiss Chard 1 cup = 290 mcg

Minerals

Minerals are nutrients your body requires to function properly. They are consumed mostly in animal and plant form. Without these minerals we would be prone to illness, and a lack of performance.

Zinc

Zinc is a trace element that is found in natural foods, fortified foods and as a dietary supplement. It aids in the breakdown of protein, fat and carbohydrates. It also assists in wound healing and immune wellbeing. Zinc deficiency is dangerous because it supports proper growth and development of the body.

An optimal daily intake for a male and female would be 8 to 11 micrograms.

Zinc is readily available in many foods we eat day to day such as:

Oatmeal cooked 1 cup = 2.3 mg

Sunflower seeds roasted ¼ cup = 1.7 mg

Lentils cooked ½ cup = 1.3 mg

Potassium

This mineral and electrolyte is important enough to make our heart beat. Yes, its functions include the transmission of nervous system signals, muscle movement, and a steady heartbeat. Potassium also lowers blood pressure and also helps our bones.

This mineral is essential to any athlete any deficiency leads to muscle cramping, vomiting and fatigue.

An optimal daily intake for a male and female would be approximately 2000 mg.

Many sports drinks include potassium, and we often see athletes eating a banana or two which also contains potassium. But these foods are also good sources:

Plums ½ cup = 637 mg

Baked Potatoes = 926 mg

Raisins ½ cup = 598 mg

Banana = 422 mg

Iron

Iron is essential for growth, development, synthesis of several hormones, and normal functioning. But it's most important function is to help hemoglobin and myoglobin (components of red blood cells and muscles) bring oxygen to all the cells that require it.

An optimal daily intake for a male would be 8 mg. and female would be 15 mg.

The following are excellent sources of iron:

Cooked lentils ½ cup = 3.30 mg

Spinach boiled ½ cup = 3 mg

Tofu ½ cup = 3 mg

Calcium

Calcium is probably the most talked about mineral and the most abundant mineral in our bodies.

Calcium is crucial for the wellbeing of bones, teeth, and muscle contraction. A deficiency in this mineral will cause poor teeth and brittle bones.

An optimal daily intake for a male and female would be 1300 mg.

Kale raw 1 cup = 100 mg

Broccoli boiled 1 cup = 62 mg

Collards boiled 1 cup = 266 mg

White beans boiled 1 cup = 161

Magnesium

Magnesium is a mineral that collaborates with calcium to help with proper muscle contraction, energy metabolism, blood clotting, and building healthy teeth and bones.

Magnesium is widely available in plants and animal foods. An optimal daily intake for an male would be 240-400 mg or female would be 250-350 mg

Good sources of magnesium are:

Brazil nuts 1 ounce = 107 mg

Pumpkin 1 ounce = 151 mg

Banana = 44 mg

Dietary Supplements

As competitors, athletes are looking to for ways to achieve their peak performance. You can complete your daily requirements your body needs with a proper diet, however many athletes turn to supplements because they believe it's a better way to optimize their health and performance. It's important to realize there is no "super pill" that can compensate for a poor diet. In order to maintain your body healthy and at its peak a balanced diet is required. But to avoid any deficiency in vitamins and minerals a dietary supplement is recommended. Supplements are meant to do exactly what their name says, supplements your regular food intake. These are not a substitute for a healthy diet or to cure any medical conditions. We would consider them as a backup, to complete the requirements of any missing vitamins or minerals in our diet.

Some supplements will definitely help you make faster improvements in your strength and composition, but before even thinking about that focus on your diet. If what you eat is not right then no supplement can help you achieve your goals.

Many vegan supplements are easily available in health stores pharmacies, supermarkets or vitamin stores. Always look at the ingredient list not all supplements are made the same, make sure you're choosing natural and organic when purchasing.

 It's also important to keep in mind what exactly you're goals are before administering these supplements. Please be mindful and consult with your doctor before taking any supplements.

Extra tips

Include foods rich in iron in your diet, like meat, dried beans, and fortified cereals. With a decreased iron diet, energy levels in athletes decrease. Females who have their menstrual cycle lose iron every month. Another way many minerals are lost is through their sweat.

Eat more Vegetables and Fruits

Not only are they packed with vitamins, minerals and phytonutrients most fruits and vegetables also contain a great sum of fiber and water. Studies have demonstrated we have a tendency to consume a consistent amount of food each day, regardless of the amount of calories contained. Water and fiber enhance the volume of foods without increasing calories. So you would be eating the same volume of food, but now with less calories and healthier.

An easy way to increase your fruit and vegetable intake is to consider each meal a **colorful one**. Aim for at least 4 or more colors with each meal, such as: carrots (orange) 1, spinach (green) 2, tomato (red) 3, potato (white) 4, lentils (brown) 5. The more colors, the more nutrients your body is acquiring.

Avoid at all times

We must have the same discipline in training as we do in our nutrition. Many of the following foods can be eaten on a rare occasion, but they should not be considered a snack or part of an everyday diet.

Foods like chips, Cheetos, sweets, cakes, cookies, carbonated sodas, fast foods, artificial colors, high fructose corn syrup, preservatives and empty calorie snacks. They will hinder performance and decrease overall good health.

Remember: **When you think you're done training, you're not done training, at least not until you've put some nutrients back into your body.**

Just as important as your workout is what you do as soon as you finish your workout. If you forget to nourish your body, you'll never get the full worth out of all the work you just put in... and what a waste that would be.

Your best performance simply won't happen if you lose focus on your body's needs for nutrients. Give your body what it needs immediately after exercising, when it's most receptive to replenishment, and it will respond wonderfully.

Chapter 7

Hydration

"Water is the driving force in all nature."
Leonardo Da Vinci

Most individuals stroll around in a dehydrated state. Athletes are no different and most of the times are dehydrated. Their performance is directly affected by their hydration level.

The world is made up of 75% water. Our bodies are 60 - 70 % water and our brains are approximately 80% water. I believe these numbers speak for themselves about the importance of water.

Water is the body's and world most important nutrient.

We send satellites to other planets in search of water, since we know this means life. People can live for weeks without food, but they can survive less than a week without water.

When the water in your body is decreased by only one percent, you immediately become thirsty. **Studies have shown that with only a one percent state of dehydration you will experience ten to twelve percent decrease in performance.** Now, that's a big difference!

When this decrease is elevated to five percent the body becomes hot and tired, muscle strength and endurance decreases even further. At 10 percent the person becomes delirious and has blurry vision. A decrease of 20 percent and the person dies. Yes, that's how important water is to our bodies.

To put these numbers into perspective let's see how much water different tissues in our bodies are made up of:

-Heart = 79% water

-Brain = 74% water

-Blood = 83% water

-Muscle = 75% water

-Skin = 72% water

- Bone 22% water

After seeing just how much water is in our body let's focus on the purpose it serves.

- Regulates body temperature. Our body has an inner heating and cooling system. Through a process of evaporation, sweat is released through the skin. This release lowers the body temperature to avoid overheating.

- Keeps your body moist. Water keeps your eyes moist when you blink, saliva in your mouth, lubricates your joints and spinal cord and keeps your brain functioning properly.

- Transport nutrients around the body. Water is the body's transportation service. It allows nutrients and oxygen into the cells to reach all areas of the body.

- It helps carry waste products away. Water lessens the burden of the kidneys and liver by flushing waste products away. The excretory system does not allow waste to build up in the body, as they could become toxic.

- Improves concentration and performance. Our brain is 75% water a deficiency in water can cause disorientation and a lack of focus.

On the other hand with a correct hydration level concentration and performance increase significantly.

Since our bodies lose water through sweating, digestion and breathing it's important to replenish it by drinking fluids and consuming foods that have water.

The ideal amount of water you need to drink is half your body weight in ounces, this amount doesn't even include special circumstances or training. If you're training your body will require an extra 16-20 ounces per hour of training.

This amount will increase even further depending on several conditions that may affect hydration levels. We must take into account the age, gender and weight of an athlete and how much time they exercise. Conditions such as heat and humidity will require more water. Another factor to consider will be altitude. If you are at a high altitude location you will also require further hydration. Certain medical conditions also require better hydration levels.

A good measure would be to weigh yourself before practice and afterward to see exactly how much water was lost during that period. With that number we can add to the 8 glasses normally required.

Try keeping a water bottle handy. Instead of drinking it all at once, take a sip every now and then. Before you know it you will be fully hydrated.

Sweat and minerals

When an athlete exercises, the body releases heat in the form of sweat. As the sweat evaporates from the skin it cools down the body and help level the body temperature. If you have not had enough water to drink the body will begin to overheat which leads to overheating and following to more dangerous conditions. We must also factor in the intensity of the exercise, the environment, and how fit the athlete is.

Sweat is mostly water, but it contains minerals also. One of these minerals is sodium. It is important to replace this sodium with sports drinks that are low in sugar. Snacks such as salted nuts, and pretzels can also help replenish lost sodium. Clinical evidence has recognized a relationship between muscle cramping and high sodium loss. The less sodium available to the muscle the more likely the muscle is to cramp.

Sports drinks are good during a long training session but keep in mind that these drinks have a lot of sugar and empty calories. You may consider mixing water and the sports drink to a 50-50 ratio, to dilute the amount of sugar, but still replenish sodium and other minerals lost. Avoid sugary drinks such as sodas and fruit juices that are not natural as they contain high amounts of sugar.

Water will always be the best drink for your body and it contains no calories. Drink water around the day do not wait until you're thirsty to consume water. Thirst is an indicator you are already dehydrated, and is usually delayed.

Be aware, a dehydrated athlete will have slower reaction times. Their ability to think and concentrate decreases, making for an inferior performance. An athlete who has not consumed enough water will become fatigued quicker and is more prone to injuries and muscle cramps. If dehydration becomes more severe, there is a risk of heat stroke, fainting, vomiting and seizures.

Hydration must be measured to avoid any complication such as the ones mentioned above. A simple yet effective way to measure proper hydration would be through urine. Depending on the color of your urine you can identify your hydration level. If the urine is a clear to pale yellow, you are properly hydrated, continue to hydrate at your normal pace. If the urine is a bright yellow or orange you are dehydrated, and are at health risk. You need to drink water immediately.

Hydration plan

We must consider hydrating a part of the training and competition process as such we need a hydration plan. This plan will give you a clearer understanding of what, how and when to drink.

Before an event

The night before you can already begin to increase your water consumption, as well as increase sodium and electrolytes.

Approximately two hours before, hydrate with about 16 to 20 ounces of water. The goal is to prepare the body for competition.

During an event

Every break, 4 to 6 oz. of water should be consumed. This would be 4 to 6 gulps. You must also include sports drinks, consider higher amounts if the conditions are hot or the event is of high intensity. This will help maintain energy in the muscles and body.

After an event

Immediately after begin to hydrate. On average 1-2% of the body weight is lost in sweat during an intense workout. This amount must be replenished, if you are prone to heat related cramps or sweat was excessive, you may choose to add salt to the fluids or meal to recuperate the body.

It's vital to have a hydration plan to ensure your body is healthy and able to compete.

Drinking water is important for everyone, but even more so for athletes. If you wait until you're thirsty to drink water you're already too late. Your body has already signaled your brain you're dehydrated and need to drink water soon.

Many individuals are committed to their athletic goals but often overlook the easiest ways to stay healthy and fit. Staying hydrated is essential to peak performance in any sport.

Chapter 8

Dream of Winning

"If you don't eat according to your goals then don't expect to reach them" Rolsey

By now we have understood the importance of proper nutrition and hydration, after all it makes up to 70% of your performance levels. Ultimately your diet can make or break you.

Success in any field does not happen by chance. It is the result of deliberate decisions, conscious efforts, and immense persistence.

Every time you embark on a journey you first imagine your destination. Next you stop and think how you will get there. The same can be said for your nutrition.

You must establish first what it is that you want, are you looking to lose some weight, gain muscle or simple perform better? Keep in mind your final destination, being the best might require a combination of these options, the answer can be one or many.

Once you have established what you want you must establish how you will achieve your goal. This is important not only in your diet, but also in life.

In order to set on the correct path you must first know where you would like to go. Set your goals high, and strive for excellence.

When you decide you're setting your goal and decide not to follow through a certain path it's very easy to get lost. You wake up one day you decide to eat one thing, the next another and all of a sudden you simply quit. You got lost along the way and never met your final destination.

Countless of the most successful individuals in the world lay their success down to knowing what they wanted and where they were going.

Well-structured goals and strategies are the single most important base in the long-term effectiveness and sustainability of your career.

Goals need to be constantly reappraised, and refocused. In tough times even injuries might appear, not always physical, they can also be emotional. You can always adapt, your path is not set in stone, even if you must make some adjustments keep moving forward.

Challenges will appear along the way, embrace them.
Make your goals fun and engaging. This will motivate you and impulse you in the correct direction.

Be **SMART** with your goal setting.

Specific- the more specific your goals are, the easier it will be to reach them.

Measureable - if you can quantify the progress, the results will be clearer. Establish your goals so you may see your progress in numbers.

Attainable - make the goals realistic. We are boosting your confidence by every goal that you reach. We need to make these goals accessible to you; they must be challenging, but still be attainable.

Relevant - the goal must help you move in the direction of larger ideals. It must make sense.

Time bound - goals have a better chance to be achieved when there is time frame in which they must be achieved.

When establishing goals we must also consider the following suggestions.

1. Few goals. Do not overwhelm yourself with goals; select a few goals at a time. Your energy and focus is designed to concentrate on a select couple to excel.

2. Flexibility. Goals are not set in stone. They may change, adapt and evolve. Physical abilities, personal circumstances, and time constraints, may sometimes require adjusting our goals. This is not giving up on the goal, but merely adapting to any new situations which are impeding you to achieve it.

3. Difficulties. There will always be road blocks along the way. But these will only make you value your achieved goals even more. When a task is challenging, more value is automatically placed on the outcome. When something is handed to you it doesn't have the same value as when you earned it.

Keep a nutrition log

Dreams are only dreams until you write them down.
Then they become goals.

Keep a journal with you so you may write down everything you eat. No cheating on this part, even if you just had half of a beer or a chunk of chocolate. For some reason when you actually write and read all these foods you can realize what is lacking or in excess in your diet. Trust me you might be shocked. I remember the first I did it I couldn't believe the lack of protein in my diet or just little water I was drinking.

Recording your activity is a great way to motivate yourself as well by being able to look back at all the goals that have already achieved.

It is very hard for anybody to memorize every milestone, achievement or setbacks in their journey towards becoming a star this is why these must be recorded in a journal.

Another benefit of keeping a training journal would be the motivation and confidence the journal provides. It provides you with focus and belief that you have worked hard to achieve your goals.

Some individuals are superstitious and after performing well in a competition they will continue to eat the same food before competing. It's in fact a very smart thing to do.

When you train or compete well go back to your journal, what did you eat and drink that day? Repeat this and see if the results are the same. Continue to experiment until you find the winning combination for you.

These journals should be written in a calm and trusting environment. Remember to be honest and real, but at the same time maintain a positive view to the future and log in improvements and rewards.

Celebrate your triumphs!

With each goal you achieved you are one step closer to your ultimate self.

Celebrate these victories!

There is no better feeling than knowing that all those sacrifices you made have paid off. I know firsthand how tough it is to not reach for that chocolate late at night or that craving you ignored for the greater good.

Your mind and body will thank you, and slowly but surely you will become your ultimate self.

Chapter 9

Motivation

"The secret to change is to focus all of your energy not on fighting the old, but on building the new." Socrates

How many times have you changed or tried to change what you regularly eat? Many times most likely you've tried to eat better. You've gotten rid of those cookies in the kitchen and refused the cake at the office party. But after a couple of weeks or months your motivation begins to fade. Maybe you got tired of eating steamed vegetables, or was tempted by a late night of pizza and beer. You think to yourself, I will just do it one time, and just this once can't hurt. A few slip ups and you're totally derailed, physically and emotionally.

Commitment and motivation are crucial to your success. There are no cheat days on the way to success. It turns out that the key to a successful diet is not only what you eat or how much you exercise- it's your attitude.

A successful athlete understands you won't reach your goals immediately. Rome was not built in one day and neither will your goal be reached in one day. Be persistent, lasting results are a slow process and it's all too easy to give up before you reach your goal. With the right psychological tools your chances of success can be achieved.

Motivation

You have that drive inside you to reach your goal, no matter what obstacles you encounter, nothing will stop you.
With every step closer to your goal your motivation increases more and more, you want it bad.
People who have a passion for what they do will become better faster as they will enjoy putting in the long hours required. When they have a clear set of goals it's easier to stay focused and motivated.

To reach maximum motivation levels it is important to focus on why adversity must be faced, what are the goals and what are the benefits from overcoming this adversity?

As we mentioned in our earlier chapters the clearer and simpler the goals are the steps to reach them become easier and motivation is then evident.

Self-motivation comes from deep inside it's a desire to strive for greatness.

Commitment

Commitment is the ability to control one's desires and behavior. It is being able to turn down immediate pleasure and instant gratification in order to achieve long term meaningful goals.

Commitment is more than just the hours you put in. It is the discipline to put aside other pleasures and focus hard on your own improvement. It is about hard work and single mindedness. It is about immersion in your task, getting down to the basic of what you are trying to accomplish. It is about not accepting second best knowing in your heart, when something is not good enough and can and should be better.

No personal success or goal can be achieved without commitment. It is the most important trait to achieve athletic excellence, personal merits or any outstanding triumphs.

Past a certain point, you and only you can provide that intensity of will.

Persistence

In order to be successful you must be persistent. After setting your goals and knowing where you want to go, doing all you can to get there.

There will be days when you might feel like giving up, remember you're strong and you will succeed in the end. Keep moving forward no matter how small your steps might seem.

You cannot give up no matter how difficult it seems. When you lose hope or have a setback you have to get right back up and give it another try.

With the determination to become your ultimate-self there is nothing that can stop you.

Positivity

Do you feel at your top every day? Of course not. Do you always find it easy to be positive? No. You are human just like everyone else and you have to face challenges every day.

The difference is that positive individuals recognize that their thoughts influence their behavior and they have learned to control their thoughts. Positive people know that the mental strength to be positive can be trained.

Positivity can have a huge impact on the performance level of an athlete. Developing a positive mindset can lead to resilient athletes who continuously strive to improve.

It is important to also have a positive surrounding. Team members, friends and coaches must also have the correct mindset. It takes a very determined and mentally strong athlete to remain positive when surrounded with negativity. On the other hand if an athlete is submerged in a positive environment, they can achieve even better results.

With the correct mindset anything can be achieved.

Gratitude

"It's not happiness that brings us gratitude.
It's gratitude that brings us happiness."
Unknown

In a world where many take a lot for granted,
gratitude has been slowing eroding. They
expect the roof over their head, the clothes on
their back and coaches to be at their beck and
call at all times. Just a skip away from being
spoiled, there is still hope. No matter what the
situation is, there is always something to be
thankful for.

The more grateful you are for what you have,
the happier and at peace you will be. The
happier you are, clearly everything will be
better in relationships, work and performance.

But how can we learn to be grateful? It can't
really be something forced, otherwise there is
no true sense of it. Gratitude works like a
muscle. Take time to identify good fortune,
and feelings of thankfulness can increase.
Furthermore, those who are more thankful
gain more from their efforts.

Gratefulness should not be something that we see once a year in a holiday, but a constant day to day activity. An exercise I think is wonderful to apply to this would be to at least once a day ask yourself, what am I thankful for today?

Trust me you have a lot to be grateful for, beginning with the knowledge you are acquiring with this book and how fortunate you are to be able to stay fit and healthy.

The results will surprise you. Studies have found that after only three weeks, athletes have a better attitude towards work, are happier, improve their fitness performance and have greater life satisfaction.

Believe in yourself

An individual's beliefs are based on their personality, relationships and experiences they have had throughout their life. These have shaped the individual's character and his beliefs. Beliefs are deep inside in the inner core and because of this they are difficult to alter, but they can be changed with hard work.

The belief that elite athletes have in themselves seems so natural that it's easy to believe it's just something they were born with or it just appeared after all their success.

Believe in yourself and your abilities and you will succeed.

Chapter 10

Right Company

"You are the average of the 5 people you spend the most time with." Jim Rohn

Stop and look around you, who surrounds you, who guides you and who influences you? Many will say, they are their own person and they hold no resemblance to their friends or family. When in reality your profession, your culture, your habits are in fact influenced by where you were born and those around you.

Your habits will determine the kind of person you will become. Environment optimization is important because it will have a great impact on your well-being.

If you want to be a better weight trainer for example you would practice with those better than you. You could say just by being around them some of that talent will rub off on you, but replicating what they do is ideal. If they already have the winning formula why do you need to look any further?

The same holds true to anything you do in life. Want to be wealthier? Hang out with wealthy people.

Want to be happy? Hang around happy people.

Want to be healthy and fit? Hang around healthy and fit people.

It really is that simple. Have you noticed that when you hang out with someone who is very positive you begin to see the world differently, you too begin to have a more positive outlook on life.

You're trying to get ahead and improve yourself, you've taken steps to set yourself up with success. You're in great shape both physically and mentally.

Sometimes it might not be easy to get rid of bad company, maybe you have some childhood friends who aren't the best influence but they've been you're friends for a long time.

These friends are not looking out for what's best for you. When they pull you away from what you should be doing to advance just to hang out or have a beer, it can cause you to become unbalanced. If you're not achieving your personal goals, you need to find a balance, and you're friends need to be more supportive.

Some friends plain and simple don't want to see you succeed, it reminds them that they are not succeeding in their own lives. They want to keep you around them, at the same unsuccessful level as they are.

Shake them off, and start hanging out with people who you admire. Eating healthy is not an easy task, but it can be made easier with a support group.

- Become friends with the people that you wish to replicate. Go to lunch with them, see where they go for lunch, and what they eat. You might learn something new.

- You will stay motivated by surrounding yourself with these successful athletes. Soon enough you will realize you too can achieve your goals with hard work and persistence.

- Share your thoughts and information with these successful athletes. Together you can brainstorm about different diets and fitness programs. You might be surprised at how knowledgeable your peers can be.

- They will not let you quit. Successful athletes understand we all feel like quitting some days. But together you can push past these days onto better ones.

Ultimately you acquire the habits from those who surround you. What kind of habits you wish to acquire depends only on who surrounds you.

Chapter 11

Recipes

"You don't have to cook fancy or complicated masterpieces – just good food from fresh ingredients." Julia Child

These are several of my favorite recipes that I am sharing with you, feel free to adapt and expand these recipes with other vegan foods. Be creative with your meals, mix and match foods. Think of your favorite meals and combine them into something great. Try new foods you've never tried before, you might be surprised.

Nature provides us with so much variety with textures, flavors and colors, we are extremely lucky to be able to enjoy it all.

In this chapter you will find a total of 50 recipes: 10 for breakfast, 10 for lunch, 10 for dinner, 10 for snacks and 10 for dessert.

I hope you enjoy them all!

Breakfast recipes

1. Coconut yogurt with Chia seeds

Ingredients:

1 cup of plain coconut yogurt

½ cup of strawberry coconut yogurt

½ cup of coconut cream

1 tbsp of soft tofu puree

1 tbsp of strawberry extract

3 tbsp of brown sugar

Preparation:

Combine the ingredients in a blender for 30-40 seconds, until smooth mixture. Let it stand in the refrigerator for about an hour before serving.

2. Ginger omelet

Ingredients:

½ cup of soft tofu puree

2 tbsp of olive oil

1 tsp of grated ginger

1/5 tsp of pepper

¼ tsp of sea salt

Preparation:

Tofu puree is a perfect substitution to eggs. ½ cup of soft tofu puree is a replacement for about 2 eggs.

Beat the tofu puree with a fork. Add ginger and pepper. Mix well and fry in olive oil, over a medium heat, for about 4-5 minutes. Season with sea salt to taste and serve warm.

3. Apple muesli with walnuts

Ingredients:

½ cup of ground walnuts

2 large apples

3 tbsp of flax seeds

3 tbsp of brown sugar

1 ¼ cups of coconut water

1 ¼ cups of plain soy yogurt

1 cup of rolled oats

2 tablespoons of mint leaves

Preparation:

Wash and peel the apples. Cut them into bite size pieces and place in a large bowl. Add soy yogurt, walnuts, flax seeds, rolled oats, mint and coconut water in the bowl and stir well. Leave the mixture in the fridge overnight.

Top with agave before serving.

4. Almond shake

Ingredients:

1 cup of almond milk

1 cup of soy milk

½ cup of tofu puree

1 tsp of cinnamon

1 cup of strawberries

½ cup of ground almonds

1 tsp of almond extract

Preparadion:

Combine the ingredients in a blender and mix well for 30 seconds. You can add a handful of ice cubes, but this is optional. Serve cold and store in the refrigerator.

5. Sweet walnut bread

Ingredients:

1 tbsp of agave

½ cup of ground walnuts

2 cups of almond flour

1 tbsp of vanilla extract

1 cup of tofu puree

½ tsp of sea salt

1 teaspoon of baking soda

2 tbsp of coconut oil

Preparation:

Put the agave, tofu puree, walnuts and vanilla extract in the food processor and mix well for 40 seconds.

Pour the mixture in a bowl and add flour, baking soda and salt. Stir well with a fork or even better with an electric stick mixer to get a smooth dough.

Pour the coconut oil over a baking sheet. Preheat the oven to 250 degrees. It takes about 40 minutes for bread to start rising. When it does, remove it from the oven and let it stand for at least 2 hours before eating.

The sweet taste of this bread is perfect for breakfast.

6. Almond pancakes

Ingredients:

1 cup of oats

½ cup of minced almonds

½ cup of tofu puree

1 cup of almond milk

½ cup of water

salt

cinnamon to taste

1 tbsp of oil

Preparation:

Make a smooth dough with oats, almonds, tofu puree, almond milk, salt and water, using an electric mixer. Add some cinnamon to taste – ¼ tsp will do the job. Fry over a medium heat for about 3-4 minutes on each side, or until nice light brown color. Depending on your taste, you can top them with strawberry syrup, fresh blueberries, banana slices, etc.

7. Hazelnuts & fruit shake

Ingredients:

1 small apple, peeled and cut

1 small orange, peeled and cut

½ glass of water

1 tbsp of hazelnuts, minced

1 tbsp of almonds, chopped

2 tbsp of silken tofu

½ cup of ice cubes

Preparation:

Combine the ingredients in a blender for 30-40 seconds. Drink cold.

8. Breakfast mousse

Ingredients:

½ cup of blueberries

¼ cup of strawberries

½ glass of coconut milk

1 tbsp of coconut cream

1 tbsp of soft tofu

1 tbsp of vanilla extract

cinnamon to taste

Preparation:

Beat the tofu, coconut cream and coconut milk with a fork. It will take about 5 minutes to get a nice, smooth mousse. Pour this mousse in a blender, add blueberries, strawberries and mix for 20 seconds. Add some cinnamon and vanilla extract before serving. Keep in the refrigerator.

9. Quinoa smoothie

Ingredients:

1 cup of quinoa, cooked

1 banana

½ cup of strawberries

1 cup of coconut yogurt, Greek style

1 cup of coconut milk

1 tsp of ground vanilla sticks

1 tbsp of sugar

Preparation:

Combine the ingredients in a blender and mix for few minutes, until smooth mixture. Allow it to cool in the refrigerator for a while.

10.   Peanut butter oats

Ingredients:

1 cup of oats, cooked

1 cup of unsweetened almond milk

2 tbsp of organic peanut butter

1 tbsp of strawberry syrup

1 tsp of cinnamon

Preparation:

Place the ingredients in a bowl and stir well until you get a nice, smooth mixture. If necessary, add some water. Pour this mixture in a tall glasses and leave in the refrigerator overnight.

Lunch recipes

1. Vegan couscous

Ingredients:

1 cup of instant couscous

2 large carrots

½ tsp of dried rosemary

1 cup of green beans, cooked and drained

10 green olives, pitted

1 tbsp of lemon juice

1 tbsp of orange juice

1 tbsp of orange zest

4 tbsp of olive oil

½ tsp of salt

Preparation:

Wash and peel carrots. Cut into thin slices.
Heat up 2 tbsp of olive oil in a large pan over

medium heat. Add carrots and cook, stirring constantly. It should be tender after about 10-15 minutes. Add rosemary, green beans, olives and orange juice. Mix well. Continue to cook and stir occasionally.

Combine lemon juice with 1 cup of water. Add this mixture to a saucepan and mix with 2 tbsp of olive oil, orange zest and salt. Allow it to boil and add couscous. Remove from heat and allow it to stand for about 15 minutes.

Pour these two mixtures into a large bowl and mix well with a tablespoon.

2. Grilled avocado in curry sauce

Ingredients:

1 large avocado, chopped

¼ cup of water

1 tbsp of ground curry

2 tbsp of olive oil

1 tsp of soy sauce

1 tsp of chopped parsley

¼ tsp of red pepper

¼ tsp of sea salt

Preparation:

Heat up olive oil in a large saucepan, over a medium temperature. In a small bowl, combine ground curry, soy sauce, chopped parsley, red pepper and sea salt. Add water and cook for about 5 minutes, over a medium temperature. Add chopped avocado, stir well and cook for another few minutes, until all the liquid evaporates. Turn off the heat and cover. Let it stand for about 15-20 minutes before serving.

3. Tofu fried vegetables

Ingredients:

½ cup of soft tofu

1 small onion

1 small carrot

1 small tomato

2 medium red peppers

salt to taste

1 tbsp of olive oil

Preparation:

Wash and pat dry the vegetables using a kitchen paper. Cut into thin slices or strips. Heat up the olive oil over a medium temperature and fry the vegetables for about 10 minutes, stirring constantly. Add salt and mix well. You want to wait until the vegetables soften, then add soft tofu. Stir well. Fry for another 2-3 minutes. Remove from the heat and serve.

4. Leek with seitan cubes

Ingredients:

2 cups of trimmed leeks

1 cup of seitan, cut into cubes

olive oil

thyme leaves for decoration

salt and red pepper to taste

Preparation:

Cut the leeks into small pieces and wash it under cold water, day before serving. Leave it overnight in a plastic bag.

Heat the oil in a large pan, over a medium temperature. Add seitan cubes and fry for about 15 minutes. Add leaks, mix well and fry for another 10 minutes on a low temperature. Remove from the saucepan and allow it to cool. Decorate with thyme leaves. Add salt and pepper to taste

5. Eggplant casserole

Ingredients:

2 large eggplants

1 cup of tempeh, sliced

1 medium onion

2 tbsp of oil

¼ tsp of pepper

2 small tomatoes

1 tbsp of dried parsley

½ cup of soft tofu, pureed

3 tbsp of bread crumbs

1 cup of soy milk

½ cup of soy cream

Preparation:

Grease the baking pan with oil. Preheat the oven at 350 degrees. Peel the eggplants and cut them lengthwise into thin slices. Layer eggplant slices in a baking pan. Peel and cut the onion and tomatoes into thin slices. Make another layer in a baking pan. Spread the tempeh slices on top.

Combine bread crumbs with soy milk, pureed soft tofu, soy cream, parsley and pepper in a large bowl. Whisk well until smooth mixture. Pour this mixture on top of your casserole and bake for about 20 minutes.

Cut into 6 equal pieces and serve.

6. Seitan burritos

Ingredients:

1 cup of cooked green beans

1 pound of seitan, chopped

1 cup of soft tofu

½ cup of chopped onions

1 tsp of ground red pepper

1 tsp of chili powder

6 whole grain tortillas

Preparation:

Combine seitan with ground red pepper, chili powder and onions in a frying pan. Stir well for 15 minutes on a low temperature. Remove from the heat.

Mix soft tofu with green beans in a blender. Mix well for about 30 seconds. Add the tofu mixture to the seitan. Divide this mixture into 6 equal pieces and spread over tortillas. Wrap and serve.

7. Chia seeds bread

Ingredients:

3 cups of buckwheat flour

½ cup of canned pumpkin puree

1 cup of minced chia seeds

warm water

salt

½ pack of dry yeast

Preparation:

Mix flour, canned pumpkin puree and chia seeds with salt and yeast. Add warm water and stir until smooth dough. Let it stand in a warm place for about 30-40 minutes. Sprinkle with cold water and bake in preheated oven, at 350 degrees for about 40 minutes, until nice gold brown color. Remove from the oven, cover with a kitchen napkin and allow it to cool.

8. Grilled green peppers

Ingredients:

2 green peppers

3 tbsp of olive oil

2 cloves of garlic

chopped parsley

1 tbsp of soy sauce

¼ tsp of sea salt

¼ tsp of pepper

Preparation:

First you want to prepare the sauce. In a small bowl, combine 3 tbsp of olive oil with garlic, chopped parsley, soy sauce, salt and pepper. Mix well. Spread the sauce over peppers and fry in a barbecue pan on a medium temperature for about 10-15 minutes. Stir constantly.

Serve warm.

9. Zucchini slices with garlic

Ingredients:

1 large zucchini

4 cloves of garlic

1 tbsp of olive oil

¼ tsp of salt

Preparation:

Peel and cut zucchini into thick slices. Chop garlic and fry it for few minutes in olive oil, until nice gold color. Add zucchini and fry for another 10 minutes on a medium temperature. Sprinkle with some chopped parsley before serving. Salt to taste.

10.   Baked mushrooms in tomato sauce

Ingredients:

1 cup of button mushrooms

1 large tomato

3 tbsp of olive oil

2 cloves of garlic

1 tbsp of fresh basil

salt and pepper to taste

Preparation:

Wash and peel tomato. Cut in small pieces. Chop garlic and mix with tomato and fresh basil. Heat up the olive oil in a saucepan and put tomato in it. Add ¼ cup of water, mix well and cook for about 15 minutes, on a low temperature, until the water evaporates. Stir constantly. After about 15 minutes, when all the water has evaporated, remove from heat.

Wash and drain mushrooms. Place them in small baking dish and spread tomato sauce over it. Salt and pepper to taste.

Preheat the oven to 300 degrees and bake for about 10-15 minutes.

Dinner recipes

1. Avocado tofu

Ingredients:

3 medium ripe avocados, cut in half

1 cup of soft tofu

3 tbsp of olive oil

2 tsp of dried rosemary

salt and pepper to taste

Preparation:

Preheat oven to 350 degrees. Cut avocado in half and remove the flesh from the center. Place 1 tbsp of soft tofu in each avocado half and sprinkle with rosemary, salt and pepper. Grease the baking pan with olive oil and place the avocados. You want to use a small baking pan so your avocados can fit tightly. Place in the oven for about 15-20 minutes.

2. Seitan and spinach omelet

Ingredients:

½ cup of soft tofu, pureed

½ cup of cannellini beans, pureed

1 cup of fresh spinach

5 thick slices of seitan

¼ cup of soy milk

1 tbsp of olive oil

1/8 tsp of ground red pepper

¼ tsp of salt

Preparation:

Grease the frying pan with olive oil. Heat up over to medium-high heat. Meanwhile, whisk together pureed soft tofu, pureed cannellini beans, spinach and soy milk. Pour into pan and stir for 3-4 minutes. Add seitan slices, ground pepper and salt. Turn off heat, but keep the pan on burner until seitan is heated.

3. Pureed prunes whites with tofu

Ingredients:

½ cup of pureed prunes

1 cup of pureed soft tofu

¼ cup of soy milk

1 tbsp of oil

salt to taste

Preparation:

Combine pureed prunes with pureed soft tofu. Mash well with a fork and add some salt to taste – about ¼ tsp will be enough. Grease the frying pan with oil. Heat up over to medium-high heat. Pour this mixture into a frying pan and fry for 3-4 minutes, stirring constantly.

4. Sweet potatoes with agar powder

Ingredients:

4 medium sweet potatoes, peeled

2 tbsp of plain agar powder

2 medium onions, peeled

1 tbsp of ground garlic

2 tbsp of olive oil

½ tsp of sea salt

¼ tsp of ground pepper

Preparation:

First you need to disolve 2 tbsp of plain agar powder in 2 tbsp of water. Whip well and place in the refrigerator for 15 minutes.

Preheat your oven to 350 degrees. Spread the olive oil over a medium sized baking sheet. Place the potatoes on a baking sheet. Bake for about 40 minutes. Remove from the oven and allow it to cool for a while. Lover the oven heat to 200 degrees.

Meanwhile, chop the onions into small pieces. Take the agar powder out of the fridge. Whip well again. This will give you an egg whites substitute. Cut the potatoes into thick slices and place them in a bowl. Add chopped onions, egg whites, ground garlic, sea salt and pepper. Mix well.

5. Cranberry oatmeal

Ingredients:

1 cup of fresh cranberries

2 cups of rolled oats

1 tbsp of pumpkin seeds

1 medium apple, cut into slices

1 cup of almond Greek yogurt

½ cup of almond cream

½ cup of maple syrup

Preparation:

Preheat the oven to 350 degrees. Spread the pumpkin seeds in a baking sheet and toast for about 5-6 minutes. You want a nice lightly brown color.

Boil the cranberries over a high temperature. Cook until they burst. Add the oats, almond cream, apple slices and stir well. Cook for another 7 minutes, or until the oats are cooked. Stir in the pumpkin seeds. Remove from the heat and let it stand for 10 minutes. Serve cold with the almond yogurt and maple syrup.

6. Chia seeds pate

Ingredients:

½ cup of chia seeds powder

¼ cup of chia seeds

½ cup of soft tofu, pureed

3-4 cloves of garlic

¼ cup of soy milk

1 tbsp of mustard

¼ tsp of salt

Preparation:

Chop the garlic and mix with mustard. In a large bowl, combine soft tofu with soy milk, salt, chia seeds powder and chia seeds. Mix well and add garlic and mustard. Allow it to stand in the refrigerator for about an hour before serving. It can be kept in the refrigerator up to 10 days.

7. Soft tofu with green peppers

Ingredients:

½ cup of soft tofu, pureed

2 small green peppers, chopped

¼ tsp of red pepper

¼ tsp of sea salt

1 tbsp of olive oil

Preparation:

Combine soft tofu with red pepper and sea salt and mix well using a fork.

Heat up the olive oil over to medium-high heat and fry the chopped green peppers for about 10 minutes. Add tofu, stir well and fry for another 3 minutes. Remove from the heat and serve.

8. Walnuts and strawberries salad

Ingredients:

½ cup of ground walnuts

2 cups of fresh strawberries

1 tbsp of strawberry syrup

2 tbsp of coconut cream

1 tbsp of brown sugar

Preparation:

Wash and cut the strawberries into small pieces. Mix with ground walnuts in a bowl. In a separate bowl, combine strawberry syrup, coconut cream and brown sugar. Beat well with a fork and use to top the salad.

9. Apple salad recipe

Ingredients:

1 large apple

1 cup of chopped spinach

1.5 cup of soy cream

1 tbsp of apple juice

½ cup of canned lentil

1 tsp of apple vinegar

Preparation:

Wash and peel the apple. Cut it into thin slices. Use a large bowl to combine the apple with other ingredients. Season with apple vinegar and serve cold.

10.   Spinach omelet

Ingredients:

½ cup of pureed prunes

1 cup of baby spinach leaves, chopped

1 tbsp of onion powder

¼ tsp of ground red pepper

¼ tsp of sea salt

1 tbsp of tofu, grated

1 tbsp of flaxseed oil

soy milk, optional

Preparation:

Combine pureed prunes with baby spinach leaves and grated tofu. Beat well with a fork. Season with onion powder, red pepper and sea salt.

If your mixture is too thick, you can add some soy milk.

Heat up the olive oil over a medium heat. Add egg mixture and fry for 2-3 minutes.

Spread this mixture over a baking sheet and bake for another 15-20 minutes at 200 degrees.

Dessert recipes

1. Chocolate bars

Ingredients:

1 cup of oat flakes

3 tbsp of natural cocoa powder

3 tbsp of peanut butter (choose organic peanut butter)

1.5 cup of almond milk

2 tbsp of brown sugar

baking spray

Preparation:

Chocolate protein bars are very easy to prepare. They are healthy and tasty at the same time. Mix the ingredients until you get a slightly sticky mass. Be patient – this might take some time (approximately 15 minutes). Use containers for chocolate bars (if you don't have these, soy cream containers will do the job) and lightly spray them with baking spray. Always choose non-fat baking sprays when preparing these chocolate bars. Divide the mixture into eight equal parts and fill the containers. Leave in the refrigerator overnight. If you like, you can sprinkle some more brown sugar on top of your chocolate bars.

2. Creamy banana delight

Ingredients:

1 glass of oat milk

¼ cup of silken tofu

1 tbsp of coconut flour

1 large banana

2 tbsp of brown sugar

Preparation:

Peel and cut banana into bite size pieces.

Make this creamy smoothie by mixing oat milk, silken tofu, coconut flour, banana and sugar in a blender for 30-40 seconds.

Pour into tall glasses and allow it to cool in the refrigerator before serving.

3. Vanilla shake

Ingredients:

1 glass of almond milk

1 tsp of vanilla extract

1 tbsp of minced pumpkin seeds

½ cup of soft tofu

1 tbsp of almond cream

¼ tsp of cinnamon

1 tsp of sugar

Preparation:

Mix well the ingredients in a blender for 30 seconds. Serve cold.

4. Coconut milk pancakes with strawberries

Ingredients:

1 glass of coconut milk

½ cup of soft tofu

1 glass of water

½ tsp of salt

1 cup of buckwheat flour

½ cup of ground walnuts

½ cup of strawberries, chopped

oil for frying

Preparation:

Mix well coconut milk, soft tofu and water in a large bowl, using an electric mixer. Add flour and salt and mix well with a stick blender to get a smooth dough. Now you want to add ground walnuts. Heat up the oil over a medium temperature. Make a pancakes with

¼ cup of dough. Fry in hot oil until gold brown on both sides. Top with strawberries.

5. Crunchy almond delight

Ingredients:

1 cup of coconut yogurt, Greek style

½ cup of frozen blueberries

¼ cup of whole almonds

1 tbsp of sugar

Preparation:

Combine the ingredients in a blender and mix for 30 seconds. Pour the mixture into tall glass and leave in the freezer for about an hour.

6. Banana pancakes

Ingredients:

1 cup of sliced banana

½ cup of rice flower

½ cup of soy milk

½ cup of almond milk

3 tbsp of brown sugar

1 tsp of vanilla extract

½ cup of soft tofu, pureed

½ cup of almond cream

cooking spray

Preparation:

Combine banana slices, rice flour, soy milk and almond milk in a bowl and mix with an electric mixer until smooth mixture. Cover it and let it stand for 15 minutes.

In another bowl, mix the almond cream with sugar, vanilla extract and pureed soft tofu. Beat well with a fork, or even better with an electric mixer. You want to get a foamy mixture. Set aside.

Sprinkle some non-fat cooking spray on a frying pen. Use ¼ cup of banana mixture to make one pancake. Fry your pancakes for about 2-3 minutes on each side. This mixture should give you 8 pancakes.

Spread 1 tbsp of almond cream mixture over each pancake and serve.

7. Mocha smoothie

Ingredients:

1 cup of ice cubes

1 tbsp of grated dark chocolate (80% of cocoa, vegan)

1 tbsp of cocoa

½ cup of almond milk

1 cup of coconut milk

½ cup of coconut cream

1 tsp of instant mocha

Preparation:

Mix the ingredients in a blender and blend thoroughly. Pour in tall glasses and serve cold.

8. Almond parfait

Ingredients:

2 tbsp of grated dark chocolate (80% of cocoa, vegan)

2 cups of almond milk

2 tbsp of almond cream

½ cup of pureed soft tofu

1 tbsp of brown sugar

½ cup of toasted almonds

Preparation:

Gently warm the almond milk over a low temperature. Add almond cream and stir well. You don't want it to boil! Remove from the heat and add chocolate. Stir until the chocolate melts. Set side and allow it to cool for a while. Now add pureed soft tofu, sugar and almonds. Stir well for several minutes and pour into tall glasses. Freeze overnight and serve.

9. Homemade vanilla cream

Ingredients:

1 cup of coconut cream

½ cup of coconut milk

1 tbsp of brown sugar

1 tsp of natural vanilla powder

1 tsp of vanilla extract

¼ tsp of cinnamon

Preparation:

Mix ingredients with a stick blender for few minutes. Leave in refrigerator overnight.

10.   Cherry ice cream

Ingredients:

½ cup of frozen cherries

½ cup of frozen almond yogurt

½ cup of almond cream

¼ cup of almond milk

1 tsp of cherry extract

1 tbsp of brown sugar

1 tbsp of whipped soy dessert topping

Preparation:

Put cherries, almond cream, almond milk and sugar in a blender for 30 seconds, until you get a smooth mixture. Meanwhile, combine cherry extract with frozen almond yogurt and whipped dessert topping in a small bowl.

Pour both mixtures in tall glasses, so that the frozen almond yogurt is on top. Leave in the refrigerator overnight.

Snack recipes

1. Tofu sandwich

Ingredients:

½ cup of soft tofu

1 cup of regular tofu, sliced

1 tsp of dried parsley

8 thin slices of whole grain bread

salt to taste

1 medium tomato (optional)

Preparation:

Cut tofu into thin slices. Layer 1 tbsp of soft tofu on top of the bread and top with the tofu, sliced. Sprinkle with dried parsley.

You can make another layer with tomato slices, but this is optional.

2. Avocado puree with berries

Ingredients:

1 cup of avocado puree

1 cup of wild berries

½ cup soft tofu, pureed

1 tbsp of agave

1 tsp of brown sugar

Preparation:

Combine the ingredients in a large bowl. Beat well with a fork. Let it stand in the refrigerator overnight. This creamy mixture goes perfectly with a whole grain toast.

3. Chia seeds with coconut yogurt

Ingredients:

1 cup of coconut yogurt, Greek style

3 tbsp of chia seeds

1 tsp of ground almonds

1 tbsp of brown sugar

Preparation:

Chia seeds are very popular because of their nutritional values. There is a reason why they're called 'superfood'. Add this high quality ingredient into your coconut Greek yogurt and you will have a great meal full of proteins and other valuable ingredients.

For this easy recipe, combine 3 tbsp of chia seeds with 1 cup of coconut Greek yogurt, 1 tsp of ground almonds and 1 tbsp of brown sugar. Use a fork or an electric mixer to get a smooth mixture. Allow it to cool in the refrigerator for about 30-40 minutes before serving.

4. Tofu toast

Ingredients:

4 slices of whole grain bread

½ cup of soft tofu, pureed

1 cup of baby spinach, chopped

½ cup of tofu, sliced

2 tbsp of extra virgin olive oil

1 tsp of dried parsley

Preparation:

Combine tofu with parsley and beat well with a fork in a bowl. Cut tofu into small cubes and add them to the bowl. Grease the frying pan with olive oil. Heat up over to medium-high heat and fry baby spinach for several minutes, stirring constantly. Add tofu mixture and fry for several more minutes.

Put the bread in the toaster for 2 minutes. Spread this mixture over the bread. Eat while warm and crunchy.

5. Mixed fruit shake, Greek style

Ingredients:

3 cups of coconut yogurt, Greek style

½ cup of soft tofu, pureed

1 cup of fresh apple juice

½ cup of frozen mango, chopped

½ cup of frozen pineapple, chopped

1 tbsp of sugar

1 tbsp of natural orange extract

Preparation:

Combine the ingredients in a blender and mix for 30-40 seconds. Serve cold.

6. Wild berries smoothie

Ingredients:

1 cup of almond milk

½ cup of water

½ cup of almond puree

½ cup of mixed wild berries, frozen

1 banana

½ cup of ice cubes

1 tbsp of brown sugar

½ tsp of cinnamon

Preparation:

Combine the ingredients in a blender for few minutes. Allow it to cool in the refrigerator for about an hour before serving.

7. Soft tofu with tumeric

Ingredients:

1 cup of soft tofu, pureed

1 tbsp of flaxseed oil

1 tsp of ground tumeric

salt and pepper to taste

Preparation:

Grease the frying pan with flaxseed oil. Heat up over to medium-high heat. Meanwhile, whisk together pureed soft tofu and tumeric. Add some salt and pepper to taste and fry for few minutes, stirring constantly.

8. Quick almond snacks

Ingredients:

3/4 cup of ground almonds

1/4 cup of grated coconut

3/4 cup of goji berries

1 cup of coconut milk

½ glass of water

1 tsp of vanilla extract

1 tsp of grated orange peel

1 tsp of chili powder

3 tbsp of grated dark chocolate with 85% of cocoa

Preparation:

First you need to mix the grated orange peel with chili, vanilla extract and coconut milk. Cook on a low temperature for 10-15 minutes. Allow it to cool. Meanwhile, mix the almonds, grated coconut, goji berries and water in a blender for few minutes. Add the cooled mixture of chili, vanilla extract, orange peel and coconut milk and mix for another 1-2 minutes. Pour the mixture into round molds and sprinkle with dark chocolate on top. Let it stand in the refrigerator for few hours.

9. Coconut cream and avocado puree

Ingredients:

½ cup of coconut cream

1 cup of coconut milk

½ avocado

salt

Preparation:

Add a pinch of salt to coconut cream and leave in the refrigerator for about 30 minutes. Place in a blender. Cut avocado into small pieces and add to the blender. Add coconut milk and blend for 30 seconds. This puree should be eaten right away.

10. Pumpkin seeds and strawberries shake

Ingredients:

1 cup of strawberries

1 glass of soy milk

¼ cup of pumpkin seeds

¼ cup of ground hazelnuts

1 tbsp of coconut cream

1 tbsp of pureed soft tofu

2 tbsp of brown sugar

Preparation:

Combine the ingredients in a blender for 30-40 seconds. Pour in tall glasses and let it stand in the refrigerator for about 30 minutes. Serve cold.

CPSIA information can be obtained
at www.ICGtesting.com
Printed in the USA
LVHW082332161219
640742LV00020B/2382/P